CW01521695

MAID
in SA

MAID in SA

30 Ways to Leave
your Madam

Zukiswa Wanner

(Who is still looking for her white helper –
The cleaning, cooking and homework type.
Not a shrink.)

JACANA

First published by Jacana Media (Pty) Ltd in 2013

10 Orange Street
Sunnyside
Auckland Park 2092
South Africa
+2711 628 3200
www.jacana.co.za

© Zukiswa Wanner, 2013

All rights reserved.

ISBN 978-1-4314-0896-2

Cover design by publicide
Set in Sabon 10.5/16pt
Printed by Ultra Litho (Pty) Ltd, Johannesburg
Job no. 002055

See a complete list of Jacana titles at www.jacana.co.za

Author's note

I would like to give a nod to South African humourists of my generation who I may or may not have borrowed from as I wrote this work through the stories they have told me or something they have written. Yes, I am talking to you Ndumiso Ngcobo, Makgano Mamabolo, and that whip-wielding loss to *Sunday Times*, Ben Trovato. As well as that oke who wrote *The Racist's Guide to the People of South Africa* (since we haven't been formally or informally introduced, may I just call you oke?). Thanks are also due to many of Angela Makholwa's domestic helpers and to Ange herself for employing them so I could get material for this book. And yes, this shout-out is so that she won't ask for any share of the royalties...

Finally, I need to say this: **this is a work of non-fiction. Any similarities to madams, baases, domestic workers and domestic incidences *imagined* is coincidental. Names have been changed to protect the children.**

PART I

"*I am human too, madam. R.E.S.P.E.C.T*"

– A HELPER'S GUIDE TO MADAMS

The Rich Madams

*L*et's begin with where the money's at. Anywhere else in the world, 'old money' refers to families that have been in the money for over a century. That is not quite the definition by South African standards. In Mzansi, we set our own standards. We're just cool and above everyone else's definitions like that. By South African standards, 'old money' is anyone who made their money before 1994 and 'nouveau riche' is anyone who made their money after 1994. When they are black you stretch it further and say that the 'nouveau riche' is the person who made money in the tenderpreneur days of the late-Mbeki or early-Zuma years. Of course, the old money concept is also determined by which race you are talking about. The table on the following page illustrates this.

White South Africa		Black South Africa	
Old Money	Nouveau Riche	Old Money	Nouveau Riche
Oppenheimers	Kebbles	Maponyas	Kenny Kunene
Ackermans	Crouses	Sexwales	Mpisanes

So you look at the table above and ask, where are the Indians? Well, there are no rich Indians. When Indians are rich, they are black. Ask the Shaiks. Or the Guptas.

Now while it is true that the Maponyas had some change pre-1994, we know the Sexwales did not. So what makes the Sexwales old money while the Mpisanes and Kenny are not? And what made Kebble and Crouse nouveau riche?

Attitude, dude.

And information. So keep your eyes wide open as your read further, and make sure you *know* whether your madam is one of these types. That way, you'll know what to expect when you are employed by her.

The nouveau riche madam

When you think Kebbles, Crouses, Kenny and Mpisanes, you think 'flashy'. This is the epitome of our nouveau riche: they are consumed with 'image' and showing that they have 'arrived'. You will find this madam and her hubby or partner – beware the terminology – in Melrose Arch, Sandton, or because of proximity to 'power', often Forest Town or greater Houghton.

They have no problem swiping their credit card at a Sandton boutique so they can buy a watch for R200 000. Or throwing an all-white party that costs millions. Yes, millions. One party. And no, we won't talk about those who eat sushi off naked bodies used as platters. I mean, that is sooo 2011 and overdone, even Kenny has chucked that habit in favour of 'saving the poor'. The nouveau riche work on reputation. Because South Africa, both black and white, is in awe of rich people who look like they have so much money, they just don't know what to do with it.

They eat in expensive restaurants. And because they are not that dumb – not always – and know what their cash flow is like, they will ensure that they dine with groupies who need some networking to help out on a deal. These groupies end up picking the tab for the expensive meal and the copious amounts of Glenfiddich. Or Moët & Chandon bought to celebrate another tender. Sounds like your madam and her husband? Good. Now for a little more information you may need...

The nouveau riche madam and her husband invest in cars. They have BMW, Porsche, Mercedes, Lamborghini and whatever top-of-the-range cars you can think of. The garage at their house is like a luxury car sales floor.

Whatever money is made from a deal goes into having fun and throwing a great party because, "you only live once". Your madam wears designer clothes and shoes. She holidays in Brazil where she has gone to get a little nip-and-tuck. Where you see a poor Indian woman in Durban, she sees a potential weave. She could be half her husband's age, or if he is a clever cop, they are around the same age. They are the darlings of lifestyle editors in the media, who never question where they got their money until they become *personae non gratae*. Unwanted. Undesired, even. Mostly because the media has found someone richer, flashier, or they've been caught doing something illegal. The charm is gone. And by then, so are your wages. Be warned.

You are hired because your cousin knows them and they need a helper. You could be anyone. Your age and looks are irrelevant. That is because the nouveau riche madam is confident and does not feel threatened by anyone. You just have to be good at looking after the children and keeping them out of the way when a good party is being thrown. Which is often. The nouveau riche madam attends the Durban July, the J&B Met – any large party that you can think of, she and her husband attend and their pictures will be in the tabloid the next week showing what they were wearing. The madam never wears the same outfit twice and her husband seems to spend an equal amount of time looking at himself in the mirror. She will call you and the other helpers to her bedroom (more like studio) and ask you what you think of this or that outfit. If you express admiration for any one of them, she will pass it on to you after she has worn it once to a function. This is how you end up with designer bags, shoes and clothes that she will not dare to be seen in again. Your friends think you are lucky to be employed by these *ngamlas*. You will soon find out that maybe you are not that lucky.

The nouveau riche send their children to the most expensive private schools and during School Development Association meetings, they will be the most vocal in agreeing to raise the school fees to 'maintain standards' and keep the riff-raff out. Except that it is One Big Con. The nouveau riche generally have cash-flow problems. What looks like Money, is not always the real thing.

If you can avoid it, try not to be employed by them. That is because there is debt being serviced somewhere. They use your 'friendship' and the guilt you feel for receiving expensive designer clothes from them so as to never pay you on time. And you are not the only employee being conned. Ask all the other employees. The drivers, the receptionists, the personal assistants: they have been waiting for their money for a long, long time.

If you are wise, you will leave them because you realise after six months that you have been getting your pay in bits and pieces, even though it is not that much money for them and they always act like they can afford it. If you are not that clever, you will leave because by now SARS has done a lifestyle audit, the home is going under the hammer and the cars are grabbed by the banks because they were not fully paid for. It is then that the scales finally fall from your eyes and you realise that these folks are actually not rich, just really great pretenders at being rich.

Should you not be that clever, it means you will likely leave with nothing except your uniform and your designer gear – if you're lucky. And it is then that you will find out that they were also not paying your (and the other employees') Unemployment Insurance Fund.

CCMA? Forget about it. There are many other people standing in line to be paid, and when their property is liquidated, you may be one of the last people in line. You should just hope for Unemployment Insurance Fund as you hunt for your next job.

OLD MONEY

The homes (note the plural) of the old-moneyed are comfortable. There is generally a home in each of the major cities and a 'country home' in Franschhoek or Stellenbosch. In Gauteng, the family home will be at an estate in Randjesfontein or Kyalami. It will consist of the main house with the servants' quarters a discreet distance away, but fully furnished because the help must be happy to give good service. There may be a stable with horses that participate in the races that the nouveau riche attend in Turffontein, Durban or Cape Town. The madam or sir may attend the races themselves if their favourite horse is running. Otherwise they will not be seen at these common affairs. Because South African 'old money's' ideas of social gatherings are charity balls and fundraising teas. And madam and sir do not play golf. Everyone knows it is a sport for the nouveau riche. They play polo.

Madam and sir of the Old-Money sort call British Lords and Dames, who consider Cape Town their playground, by their first names. For this reason, you will have to be an exceptional employee to work for this lot. Your duties are specific. Here, you are not expected to cook, clean, mind the children, and all the multiple duties you undertake for the other madams and baases.

If you are a maid, you will need to know how to set the table properly. You will need to know your fish knife from your steak knife and how to starch the serviettes – this lot do not use napkins, they use serviettes – and make them appear attractive at breakfast, lunch and dinner. You also have to know the individual requirements for the table for morning tea and afternoon tea. And although you will never understand why this must be done, you will also have to know how to cut the crust off the bread when you serve the sandwiches. And know that not all sandwiches have polony. Some of them have odd things like cucumber and liver pâté. You therefore cannot have just come from some agency willy-nilly. You, dear maid, were head-hunted from the madam's favourite boutique restaurant.

Your duties entail communicating with the Malawian gardener on having a fresh flower arrangement every other day for the dinner table. If the children are young, they will have an au pair. You may know their names but they are under the care of the au pair, and your primary job is to ensure that dinner is served correctly. If they are older, you will know them because you serve them and their governess (the French woman who tutors them in French or the Chinese woman who is teaching them Mandarin so that they can be globally competitive when they join the family business) in a separate dining room during the holidays. They do not attend school in South Africa, you see. They are at Eton or other similar British public schools. You will refer to the children as Master or Miss until they are teenagers when they have silly socialist notions and they say to you, "No. No. Just call me Martin", and you do. Although, you will always know your station. It is then that they will join their parents at the big table and are allowed some wine and/or whisky. Bad table manners from the children result in the madam or sir raising their eyebrows and admonishing the children for exhibiting 'common behaviour'.

Your immediate supervisor is a cordon bleu French chef imported from France. The wine served at dinner is from the family estate in Franschhoek or Stellenbosch. You will know how to pour it properly because, after all, you were recruited from the madam's favourite boutique restaurant. Sometimes, if your service is favoured above all, your job will include travel. Madam may have a dinner party at the home in Durban, Cape Town or the country home.

Unlike all the other madams, you will know very little about this one as a person. She will never be heard yelling at you or saying cross words; she conducts herself with reserve around the hired help, i.e. you. You will catch snippets of information about her and her husband from the other employees, but none of you will have a clear portrait of her.

You will leave for one reason and one reason only:
- When you are retiring. Other than that, the pay package is great. Better than at the boutique restaurant she took you from. The work is not hectic. And you will probably get married to one of the other employees, so what reason do you have to leave?

Indian Madams

THE CONSERVATIVE INDIAN MADAM

When using South African speak in reference to South Africans of Indian origin, conservative means 'lower middle-class'. Not quite as poor as the white madams staying in Benoni or Turffontein, but not rich, and therefore not comfortable with the thought of having black friends. The only blacks this madam knows are those who work in the family business, which may or may not be at the Oriental Plaza.

When you arrive at work here, you only stay because you have to. The family home is in Fordsburg, Mayfair, Marshalltown, Crosby, or if the family is doing slightly better, Roodepoort. This family has the matriarch running everything. The paterfamilias is almost invisible except at the shop or when he is playing with the grandchildren. The person in charge here is ma. She is the one who gives you a job.

She has four sons, three of them married. If in Fordsburg, Mayfair or Marshalltown, the first two sons and their wives stay in the house. They are both in the family business. The first son, because he was groomed to be in the business, and the second son, because he did not really make a success of his life. Their wives do not work. And always seem harassed. This is because they are. While you do all the cleaning – including the bathtubs after each family member has taken a bath, because they are incapable of washing their own dirt from the bathtub – the wives do all the cooking. You are not allowed to touch the cooking because you are not Muslim and it is *haraam* for you to do so. Unless you are Muslim you are just not allowed to make the food because she is not sure of your personal hygiene. If in Roodepoort, there is enough space in the yard so extra cottages have been built for the brothers and their wives, although there are only rooms to sleep. Everyone eats in the house with ma and pa, as everyone calls them.

The third son, Ishmael, and his wife Safia have moved to middle-class neighbourhoods like Parktown, Orange Grove or even Midrand. He and his wife both work. She is a doctor and he is a pharmacist. Or vice-versa. Or maybe one of them is an accountant or a banker. He is pa's favourite son because he did something with his life. Ma does not like his wife because she took her baby away. And the sisters-in-law and the brothers think his wife puts on airs. She also looks like she drinks wine. Which is *haraam*. And why does she not have any children yet? They have been married for four years already, while between Imraan and Yusuf there are five children. She thinks she is better than everyone, is what everyone says in her absence. And sometimes they whisper it loud enough for her to hear it, when she's present.

The fourth son is studying at the University of Cape Town. He is his mother's favourite son because he looks like her brother. He stays off campus. Every Friday, there is a lot of work to be done before prayers. This is because the sisters-in-law have to cook many different foods, which are put in lunch boxes and given to the driver Bilal early on Saturday morning. You also have a lot of washing and ironing to do. This is because you have to give the freshly laundered clothes to the driver. Early Saturday morning, Bilal gets in the car and drives from Johannesburg to Cape Town with the food in coolers to deliver for the week as well as clean clothes to "darling boy Tariq who is working so hard to be a lawyer, he probably has no time to eat". This has been happening since Tariq was in first year. His girlfriend must be relieved that they can concentrate on their studies, go drinking on Long Street, and do whatever it is that young university students do. The sisters-in-law and the brothers know about the girlfriend. Brothers one and two think Tariq is just going through a phase so no-one must tell ma otherwise she may have a heart attack for nothing. Ishmael and that hoity-toity Safia have entertained the black girl at their house during the holidays. In fact, Tariq spends most of his holidays there (much to ma's annoyance).

On being employed, you are given your duties. Your duties entail waking up early in the morning and cleaning the house. There is a plate and a cup for you (both metal à la poor white madam's house). Your breakfast consists of bread and tea. The laundry is done three times a week. You would really prefer to do it five times a week so that you would not have so much to wash when you finally get to it on the designated laundry days, but this is not to be. Ma wishes you could do it twice a week as she already complains about how much soap is used up the three times you do it. There is always a lingering smell of incense in the house. Ma likes vanilla incense. She says it keeps the jinn away. And after you finish cleaning daily, you have to light some incense for each room (two for the living room).

In every room, the curtains are thick and dark and there are also lovely thick rugs in the living room, in the prayer room, in the bedrooms. You are expected to dust and clean these using a brush, and once a month you will remove them and shampoo them outside and leave them to dry. It is not because there is no vacuum cleaner in the house (there's probably a Hoover), Ma is just not sure you know how to use it and, besides, she really seems to believe that the Hoover cannot make the mats as clean as she prefers.

There is a spaza shop at the house. There have been some bricks removed in the wall to create an opening the size of a small window, where the seller can communicate with customers. The small window has a mesh wire because this is Johannesburg, and a robber can sommer come and get all the money, the sisters-in-law's jewellery, and maybe some groceries. The groceries are put through a small hole that can be pulled back and forth similar to those found in banks. You should be done with the cleaning, dusting, and on the laundry days, laundry by 11 am. At that time you are expected to go and help the younger sister-in-law at the spaza while the elder sister-in-law goes to make lunch. The husbands will come home and the elder sister-in-law will serve lunch to them and ma. On days when things are really busy at the shop, Bilal will come through and collect food to take to the shop for the husbands. Pa never comes through for lunch. He seems to prefer buying something at the Oriental Plaza. This does not amuse ma one bit, but she sighs and says it is a burden she has to bear.

After lunch, elder sister-in-law comes through and swaps places with younger sister-in-law so younger-sister-in-law can go and eat. She brings you a plate of leftovers so you can eat in between passing her things, even if they are right next to her when a customer comes in. You are never allowed to handle money. You cannot be trusted.

When younger sister-in-law comes back, you leave and go to the kitchen to start washing the dishes. There is a dishwasher. But like the Hoover, you cannot be trusted to use it. Like the Hoover, the dishwasher is there for them to use on your day off. The children will come through around this time from school or crèche and ma will dish up for them. She is particularly fond of 'my handsome two boys' as she calls them. The young girls are a nuisance, she says.

If it is a laundry day, at this time you will go and get the laundry off the line, and then start the ironing. The sisters-in-law will close up the spaza at five and then they come into the home where they will sit down to count the money with ma. They must account for each and every penny and take stock on what it is the husbands will need to bring the next day to stock up. The money is given to ma who takes it to her bedroom. And when she does this, she glances furtively at you. Don't you dare make eye contact when she does this.

The only day you are away from this house is on Sunday. It is then that you go and visit your relatives and once or twice you may bump into another helper who is also having her day off. When you start talking and you compare notes, you realise that your working life for ma is not the horror story you thought it was. In this neighbourhood, it is pretty standard, really.

Why you leave:

- You get your wages. There seems to be some unnecessary deductions for things you were not informed of in advance as ma hands you the money. "You washed your clothes. We have to take some money for your water costs and for the soap." As she chats and hands you the money, you feel like you may have to pry the money out of her hands. She is trying as much as possible to find a way not to give you anything, you think. On your next day off, you leave and take whatever you can and never come back.

- You have saved enough money during the time you worked for ma to go and start your own spaza shop back in Seshego.

- If you've been reading and paying attention to this, hopefully it's a combination of the above two points. Good luck!

The Liberal Middle-Class Indian Madam

The liberal middle-class Indian madam is Safia or one of her sisters. She is a doctor, a banker, a pharmacist, a lawyer or an academic. If she is a doctor or a pharmacist, she owns a travel clinic. She does not have black friends. That is because she does not *need* to have black friends. She *is* black. When she is with her friends they raise their eyebrows at 'these liberal whites', and talk about the neo-colonisation of Africa. She grew up thinking she was Indian back in Durban, but in her second year of university she went for a holiday to Delhi and realised that she is proudly South African. Now she cheers for Proteas whether they are playing against India or Pakistan, and even when Hashim Amla is not playing. While her family does not quite have the struggle credentials of the Meers, the Shaiks, the Pahads or Big Mac, they all know her daddy. She grew up calling them uncles and aunts and when she bumps into them at a party they will say:

"How lovely you have grown, Safia. Mo, you remember Anil's young daughter. Anil, who was the first Indian to own a shop selling bunny chow on North Beach?"

"*Ja, ja.* The best bunny chow in all of Durban I tell you. Safia, say hello to your father and tell him I miss his bunny chow."

She is at home in the neighbourhoods largely populated by the middle-class white madams or the middle-class black madams. She really likes Midrand, though. And it is out of town and a nice drive in her X5. She has fantastic single friends among her fellow black middle class but she is conservative enough to be married. She believes in having it all.

Her husband is a quantity surveyor, an actuarial

scientist, a lawyer, a banker. A real catch. He also drives a BMW. They considered personalising them but decided it would be too 'ghetto'. A word that she and her friends use often.

She did not find you at an employment agency. Neither did you go knocking on her door to get a job. You have known each other since you were children. Your mother used to work at her parents' shop and you were 'friends' since childhood, if the word friend can be used loosely. Okay, you were friends but certainly closer when you were children, less so when you became teenagers because then the differences became blatant. She was your mother's boss's daughter and even though you were invited by her kind and gentle mother to their home once or twice, you never quite felt comfortable as you did not have the right clothes. And it did not feel quite like friendship in retrospect as you had been getting her hand-me-downs.

You got pregnant at 17. Your mother asked her father to give you a job in the shop. And when Safia finally got married and had children, her mother 'suggested' to you that you may want to come to Johannesburg to help her out with the children. "You are her friend and you are family to us. There is no-one we would trust more with our grandchildren. Please Faith, you go and help out your sister." You do not really have a choice. You need the money. And you already know Safia, it really is somewhat like family. You go.

And Safia welcomes you.

Your cottage is more comfortable than most. There is a television, a fridge, a two-plate stove. One of those with the microwaves at the bottom. The pay is generous. As are the hours. Safia is keen to make you feel that you are her friend, first and foremost. She asks you whether you want anything. And will come to your cottage with a bottle of wine or some ciders. Yes, she is a practising Muslim (sometimes) and, like a few practising South African Muslims, she too stops drinking. During Ramadan. She comes to you so you can chat and gossip about old friends, old times, or just something that happened to her where she needs to speak to someone she can trust. She knows that you will not judge her. That is the type of relationship you have always had. And yet you will also give her your honest opinion on things. It is a gift for her to have you. Safia is always keen to look perfect in front of her friends and she is the one who listens to all their problems but can never quite come to share hers as she may look imperfect. She does not mind appearing imperfect to you, though.

Her husband does not quite know how to treat you. He is unsure whether you are a servile friend or a friendly servant. This becomes clear and uncomfortable when they have friends visiting. "Faith is like family to us," he will say trying to delete his bourgeois leanings. "She and Safia grew up together. We are family, aren't we Safia?" he asks turning to you. And she will say,

"Oh, Faith don't worry about washing up. I will put the plates in the dishwasher when we finish dinner. You can go ahead and rest. I would not want to be responsible for your missing *Generations*," she will add with a laugh. You are sure that they both did not mean to sound patronising but they do. And thus the line between employer and employee is demarcated. You now know your place.

She has two brilliant and respectful children that you never have to assist with homework. That is because they seem to know more than you do. They get awards. You wish your Bongiwe would get awards like they do. But your mother told you she is busy chasing boys. You hope she does not get pregnant in high school like you did.

You leave because:
- Safia has been paying for you to do some courses to improve yourself and now you have a job in one of the hotels in Durban. As a receptionist. Imagine. And you can be closer to your daughter and watch her so she does not chase boys. Not that being watching by your mother stopped YOU from teen pregnancy.
- Your current boyfriend wants to get married. Safia and her husband look so happy. You also deserve to be happy like that.

- You just miss eThekwini. At least that is what you tell her. But really working for your childhood friend is a bit awkward. It is better to go back to the shop. Her father is not your friend.

African Madams

There is only one type of black madam. The middle-class African madam. As mentioned before, the rich African madam is not counted here as she, her Indian and her white counterpart have transcended race. The middle-class African madam, on the other hand, is aware of race and, in the same way her white counterpart claims to have black friends, she goes home and says, "*eish*, these white people," in disgust.

Poor African Madams?

There are no poor African madams. Siriyas. Poor women who work and need assistance with the children usually go *emakhaya* and get one of their poorer relations to come and help out. As you are family, you will not be paid but instead will have fees paid to do a call centre course. As your poor relation cannot afford to send you to Quest or any of the big brand names that do placements, the call centre college you go to will be one of the fly-by-nights ones that do not do placements. You will discover this bit of information after the course. So while waiting for some response from all the companies you sent your CV to – which, sorry for you, may never come – you become the domestic worker de jure of your poor relation. You feel guilty because you are not contributing to all the food you eat so you wake up and get the children ready for school and then you walk them *to* school. Or, if there is a toddler, because your aunt, sister or cousin (who is generally a single mother) cannot afford to take them to pre-school, you spend the day looking after the child. You make all the meals, generally consisting of *mdoko* for breakfast, tea and bread for late brunch and then a proper supper when your aunt/sister/cousin comes back from work. Sometimes if you remain with the child, there may also be *maas* and *iphuthu* for lunch. There is not much variety to the meals. It's *pap* and cabbage. *Pap* and spinach. *Pap* and boerewors whose stuffing may or may not be beef. *Umqhusho* and gravy and, if you are lucky, boerewors. Except on Sunday. Now Sunday is the big day with the big meal. The day that the Lord has made will ensure that you too eat the meal that all your neighbours are eating after church. Rice with some curry to make it yellow and give it colour, roast chicken, roasted potatoes, butternut or pumpkin, coleslaw, potato salad and mixed vegetables. If it appears to you that there are too many carbohydrates in the meal, then you are probably not hungry enough and not happy to have a meal this special. As the chicken is a product of the no-name packs from supermarkets, everyone will have a leg or a breast.

Your aunt/sister/cousin's only hope during this period is that you will not get pregnant from one of the township boys before you get a job. You have time on your hands. You have the house to yourself while your relative is at work. You probably will get pregnant. And then, when the child is born and you have weaned and sent him or her home to stay with the parents *emakhaya*, you will come back to the city to look for a job with one of the middle-class African madams.

The Middle-Class African Madam

The middle-class African madam works for an NGO, a non-governmental organisation. Or she is in academia and lectures at one of the local universities. Maybe she used to work as a sectional editor at one of the newspapers, quit and started her own public relations company, or got hired into a corporate company as a public relations officer. If she is any of these, she probably has dreadlocks or rocks a natural hairstyle.

She could be in middle management in civil service,

in which case she may or may not have a natural hairstyle. She may be an accountant and a member of African Women Chartered Accountants. If this is so, then she has a weave because corporate South Africa is not yet ready for African women who assert themselves through their hair.

She could also be a well-heeled token African at some corporate company, a Director of Diversity or something similar, or heading one of the Chapter 9 or Chapter 11 institutions. Now the latter two would ideally have been considered a touch above middle class. Unfortunately, on account of being black, she is the most successful person in the family and, as such, has school fees to pay for all her siblings younger than her. Or she has child support to pay on behalf of her Loser older brother. Just so she can avoid a tabloid headline in *Sunday World* stating *Gender and Diversity CEO in Papgeld Drama*. When you read the article, you will of course realise that the *papgeld* drama is not hers but her brother's, and the person who is making a noise is the brother's babymama. So, to avoid such situations, she pays. Even though her brother treats her like rubbish to appease his battered ego, and when she goes home at Christmas he makes statements like, "you think because you're a CEO, you're the man of this home, heh?" Most of the time, he is either trying to fight with her or asking for money for booze or to drive her car.

With some exceptions, the middle-class African madam is a single parent/divorcee:

Which is great for you as you will have to be an epic fail before she fires you; after all, she needs consistency in her child's life (at least you are not like that stupid bastard who always claims he will come and see the child and never turns up). You know how much she needs you because once you overheard her on the phone after your leave saying:

"*Eish choms*, I have finally established that uRefilwe is an alien or a super Mary Poppins. I don't know how she manages to cope with such an energetic toddler and still finds time to keep the house clean, laundry washed and ironed, dinner cooked. When she returned, I was so exhausted and it had only been one week. Eh. Eh. Neo is so exhausting, I decided I was going to take an extra day off work and just sleep. Ja neh? I don't know how housewives who don't have helpers do it day in and day out. Or those women with four children? Ja sies."

So you know for sure; this woman needs you. When you are on your day off, she will call you to ask where the spoons or the coffee mugs in her kitchen are. Because you are both African, if you are her age or younger, she may call you by your name but she will insist that her child calls you aunt. If you are older, she will also call you aunt. The middle-class African madam prefers someone her age or older, ideally with children. This ensures that you both have something from each other. You have a regular income to send to your child(ren) and she has someone reliable that she can trust with her child(ren). She is a pretty fair employer and will pay you a good salary to ensure she keeps you. Unlike her white married counterpart, however, she will not say "your children can come through anytime." That is because she is probably staying in a townhouse complex in Midrand, Fourways, Melville or Orange Grove and there is not enough room for you, her children and your children. Additionally, she is not such a big fan of children even though she has her own. When she is home, she wants to relax. Sometimes, she will call you to tell you she is coming home late because she is meeting her friends for dinner. You will know when she rings the doorbell and walks in that she did not mean only dinner, as she returns, possibly with one of her female friends, talking too loudly and smelling like major investors of SABMiller.

But if madams can be said to be cool, she is cool. The middle-class African madam is your boss but is the closest to a boss who is a friend that you will ever have. When you first arrived and she asked you to make dinner, "there is meat in the deep freeze" and you made rice served with nicely fried bacon with tomato and onion gravy, she did not yell at you. In fact she said, "We cannot throw it away. Besides, it smells good," and she dug in with the children, only telling you after the children have gone to bed, that bacon is meat made for breakfast.

When drunk, she has revealed things to you that she should not have and you have told her not to cry. You also know which of her friends claims to be a *mzalwane,* yet has had multiple abortions; which one got fired at her work for swindling; and which one always talks highly of her husband, yet he beats her. You know who among her friends she does not really like but keeps because they have been friends since they were children. Because of this lack of boundaries, the black madam does not raise her eyebrows when you tell her that you may need to leave the house at 6 pm because one of the men in the townhouse complex invited you over for a drink. She just smiles and asks what unit he stays in so that she can verify that he is single and you will not be chased with a broom by his wife. When she verifies, she will let you go. And she will laugh with you when you return twenty minutes later in a rush, because when you rang the doorbell of this good-looking man you met at the gate who was driving a BMW, you could not see who had opened the door. When you finally looked down and found out that he was a dwarf, you ran back to the house in shock and panic. "*Hawu* 'Filwe, you didn't know? I thought you liked them short when you told me that was where you were going." To which you will both laugh. Sometimes if the child is away on holiday visiting her gogo for the weekend, she will even delete all boundaries and buy you some Hunter's Dry. Imagine.

If the child is a toddler, he/she runs to you when you get back from your day-off/leave and tells you everything that the mother did to him/her in your absence. If there are older children, you help them with homework and laugh when they try on your high-heeled shoes that you just bought from Ackermans (you hope she does not break the heel though).

If there is more than one child, the older one will be cheeky and say things to you like, "Aunty, it's not baby wipers, it's wipes. *Kunini ndikulungisa?*" You smile indulgently and shake your head because you cannot believe that this child you raised is now trying to teach you how to speak English properly. Just like the children of the white middle-class madam.

You will leave her because:
- She keeps trying to tell you how 'this government' is messing up and keeps suggesting that you get a membership card for COPE/Agang.
- You are getting married to your boyfriend. Your lovely madam will come to your wedding and bring you a big present or she will throw you a bridal shower with her friends so she can get you some things you will need for your new home.

- Your mother dies and you have to go home to take care of the family home, and your child needs someone there too.
- You got saved and her sinful ways of bringing men into the house and drinking like a prostitute conflict with the ways of you and your Lord.
- You are going to prison because you found another woman at your boyfriend's zozo, and you tried to burn this woman and her child in the house, and the unreasonable lawyers and judge called it felony as the child got second-degree burns.

If your middle-class African madam is married:
It will be quite different from working with the single one. While they both stay in Midrand or Fourways, her house is bigger. Not a townhouse at all.

Because there are two incomes, the house may be larger and therefore you may in this instance have your own cottage. If you do not, you will sleep with the children.

She may have a regular job and income like her single counterpart or she may be self-employed. If the latter, it is not too good for you as her routine is uncertain and you cannot watch African movies in peace during the day without her just arriving anytime.

The married middle-class African madam insists on discipline above all else with her workers. Her name is not Nosiviwe or Lindiwe but she is certainly a terror so you are convinced that in her last life she must have been a Minister of Defence. That is why, unlike her single middle-class counterpart, you do not get to work for her just by ringing her doorbell and asking for a job, but rather through an employment agency. She is the employer that you find yourself with if your white madam from Italy/France does not manage to place you with one of her white friends or if you come out of prison and your middle-class single black madam still gives you a glowing reference. When you meet the married middle-class madam, she will smile and be friendly but beware. If you are not to her exacting standards, you will not last long. She will ask for your references and, there and then in the agency, she will call them so she can know whether you will be able to do the work. All madams, except the overly liberal middle-class single black madam, do not want to employ cheeky workers, so when she talks to you, it is important that you do not meet her gaze but look at some point beyond her or keep your eyes lowered.

She has two children, maybe three. If she is self-employed, she drops the children at school on the way to the gym. If one of the children is under three, she will have a nanny whose sole work is to look after the child, while your work is to cook and clean the house.

If she has a regular nine-to-five job, her husband will drop the children at school. She will wake up early, take a bottle of water from the fridge and, dressed in gym clothes, she will put her work suit and toilet bag in her four-wheel drive. She will change at the gym, because going to the gym is an important part of her routine. Is she very fitness conscious? Perhaps. Or perhaps she is worried that, as you once overheard her tell her friend on the phone, "Girl I can't let myself go. There are *nyatsis* everywhere." She believes that she's got the last man in Mzansi and there are slutty, single women from everywhere waiting to take him from her, so she needs to be ultra-vigilant. It matters little that her husband is a beer-lugging man who thinks it is alright to tell her immediately when they get back from the Christmas holiday, "*Hawu* baby, are those love handles you are walking around with? Maybe you need to go to the gym," despite the fact that he has a beer-gut to die for. Or not. She will also tell you that you are expected to wear a uniform, which consists of a dress and a matching doek. You are only allowed to be out of your uniform during your day off or when you go to your cottage to sleep, which is when you put on your nightie.

When you wake up in the morning after you get breakfast ready for everyone, you will clean the en-suite Master Bedroom before any other place. This is because she needs to lock it before she goes to work, because you or the nanny may steal clothes from her walk-in cupboard.

The children will have cereal for breakfast, while, three times a week, her husband will have a full

English, sunny-side up. In the first week, you will get into conflict with her.

"We need to talk," she will say.

You will nod your head and put your head to the side humbly so that she sees you are respectful.

"I thought you and your employment agent told me you were trained?" she will say.

You will nod your head, unsure of where she is going with this. Unsure whether you are nodding to tell her to go on or whether you are nodding in agreement that yes, you were trained.

"So tell me Londiwe, if you are trained, why did you not make my husband's eggs the way I asked you to?" she will say.

You now have no idea what she is talking about.

She said he likes his eggs fried, sunny-side up, and so you gave him his egg fried. Yes, it is true that the last two times you made it, he did not eat it. You wonder what you did wrong. Did you put on too much salt? Maybe it got burnt at the bottom? But nee man, you were careful and you put enough cooking oil in the pan.

"Do you know what you are supposed to do?" she asks you.

"I am not sure," you will say.

Because you are unsure why you are in trouble in the first place.

Then she will pull you by the hand. "Give me that pan," she will say.

You will pass her the pan.

Then she will fry an egg. And leave it with the yolk still not done. Then she will say to you, "This, Londi, is sunny-side up. Now when you are told to do an egg sunny-side up, this is what you need to do." Well why did she not say that earlier? It is then that you realise that this middle-class black madam is even more white than the white people. Everyone knows that there is only one way to fry an egg. Until it is well done. Not this sunny-side up rubbish that will make you throw up from the smell of the yolk. Just looking at it as she puts it on a side plate makes you feel queasy.

"I thought you said you were trained?" she will say again before she shakes her head in disappointment and leaves with the plate to take it to her husband at the table.

You will shrug your shoulders. This madam deliberately forgets that you were trained for general work in the household and if she wants specific things in her own house, she should teach you how to do it. Not all madams want the same thing. You were trained to scramble an egg, to poach it, to boil it, to make an omelette and to fry it, but this sunny-side up? *Hayi nxa*!

The children will return from school with a regular driver that is paid monthly for that sole purpose. Samuel is his name.

For you and the nanny the temperature in the house drops when the madam arrives. As she parks her Range

Rover or some other gas-guzzler, you should have her house slippers ready and take away her shoes and her bag as she hands you the keys so you can leave them in her bedroom. "Good evening, mummy," she expects you to say when she comes in. You say it as you kneel to pick up her shoes. Sometimes she just grunts. Sometimes she does not answer at all. But let it be that one day you forget to greet her. She will remind you about it for a long time.

"So we do not greet? Did we spend the day with each other?" she says using 'we' as if she is an African President.

After you put down her bag, she will sit with her legs stretched on the couch in the living room. "Long day," she will sigh as though to herself, but really wanting you to hear. Maybe making an excuse for her lazy behaviour on arrival at home. She will ask you to make her some tea. She will drink her tea. Then after tea, she will go to her Master Bedroom, put on some casual clothes (always something to show off her figure so that her husband does not forget what he has at home when he gets there) and comes into the kitchen. In the kitchen there is a list of what should be cooked, Monday through Saturday. Just so that you do not get the preparations wrong. She will teach you how to marinade the meat (beef or lamb, because only beef or lamb can be referred to as meat), fish or chicken. But she will do the cooking when she arrives. This is because she has heard tales or knows women whose helpers bewitched their madams' husbands. She is not taking any chances. Your cooking consists of cooking for the children. She will start making dinner and ask you, "Londi, have the children done their homework?"

She is the one with all the degrees, why can't she inspect her own children's homework? You wonder. But you do not ask out aloud. She is paying your salary. And she is cooking for her husband. While drinking a glass of wine, which will become two, three or four as she looks at the clock and wonders when he will be returning home. The woman may feel a little threatened by you, so from the get-go she will try to assert her authority so that you know that she is the madam. This means there will be no such thing as sitting and watching *Generations* or anything on television with her and the family at dinner time as you may do at the single black madam's house. Indeed, you will not eat with them or anywhere around them. You have food in the cottage and when she comes through and dismisses you, you will go to the cottage you share with the nanny and there you will make your own meals. There is a hot plate in your cottage. And a small fridge.

Sometimes you feel that she seems to be more focused on keeping her husband than she is on ensuring that the children are alright. She is obsessed with being someone's wife. With an image. When she makes conversations with her visiting cousins or sisters she always finds a way of throwing in something about her husband. He is also on his best behaviour at this time. But you have seen him look at one of her sisters' bum as she is walking. He has winked at you once or twice when you are dressed all nice and you are going away for your day off. *Eish*. Men!

Her children always ensure that you know your place. You are the maid. They are the little baases or madams. It does not matter that they are black children and you are old enough to be their mother. Ubuntu and good home training is clearly lacking here. Another indication that this married middle-class black madam and her family think they are white. The other day her six year old has a friend for a sleepover. In the morning when the mother has come to pick him up, the polite and well-mannered young friend asks you, "Excuse me auntie, where are my pyjamas?" You had laundered them and they are now in the dryer. They should be done by now.

"I will go and get them for you." You say in English. Because although these children's grandparents stay in KwaMhlanga, GaMothapo or Harrismith, the parents proudly and loudly proclaim, "They only speak English."

And you overhear your madam's child as you walk away saying, "She is not your auntie, she is my maid. My mommy is your auntie. Don't call HER auntie." And then you hear the mother repeating it and chuckling to her friend about it. When the friend enquires why it is okay for her children to call you by your name, she will say, "I do not want them to be confused on who their relations are." Oh? So it's okay to call an adult who is much older than you by their name? You wonder.

Why you will leave:
- She fires you. In your first week. She asked you to handwash the baby's clothes with Sunlight. You did just that. How were you to know that she meant Sunlight washing powder and not dishwashing soap?
- She fires you. In your first week. For doing your job well. She says you removed the non-stick component of her Teflon pans. But you were only trying to prove that you can clean well.
- She nitpicks every little thing. She is never happy about anything and despite the money being pretty good, you are not happy.
- She tries to take your days off. She never offers you enough money to compensate for the times that she lets you stay with her children. Like that time when one of her children had a birthday party and she had you spraying water on the jumping castle so the children could slide into the swimming pool for four hours. Was the R200 overtime pay enough for so much work? No.
- She and her husband are insensitive. They throw parties almost every week where the amount of

alcohol they buy and drink in one weekend is more expensive than what they pay you in a month. Just last weekend they bought a bottle – you saw the receipt – one bottle of whisky for R4 000. And they finished it and had many other drinks. Your pay is R2 500 per month. You feel absolutely no qualms that after you leave they will find out that you were drinking his vodka and topping it up with water.

- She yells at you for no reason, the husband takes your side, and then she thinks you are having an affair with him and starts yelling at him. You try to tell her there is nothing going on but she slaps you, and although she comes to the cottage to apologise later, it is never going to be the same.

- The husband starts having too much conversation with you and making excuses to be around you when his wife is not around. And yes, he has brushed your bum with his hands once or twice, although he pretended he did not do it. Additionally, he is starting to come home for lunch breaks a little too often.

White Madams

*T*here are two types of white madams. The poor-white madam and the liberal middle-class white madam. There is also the rich white madam but as you already know the rich come in a different class and among the rich there is no race as the only colour they know is the colour of the Randelas. There is, however, one distinct quality of most white madams be they rich, middle-class or poor. They do not have a day job – at least not in the normal nine-to-five that other working madams may.

The Poor-White Madam

Meet the poor-white madam. She grew up and married a hustler from a similar background. This white madam is usually Portuguese or Afrikaans but every now and again you will encounter a loser of English origin. She is not Sonskyn Hoekie poor but if something terrible happens, she and her family may find themselves in this squatter camp or one similar to it. In Johannesburg, she is found in neighbourhoods originally designed for poor-whites by the apartheid regime like Benoni, Brakpan, Turffontein or the former Sophiatown-then-Triomf-then-Sophiatown again. Whereas black people move into these neighbourhoods because they are trying to move up from the township or whatever their lives were like in Congo, Zimbabwe or Nigeria, this madam and her family will never become rich – unless they join the ANC, become token whites in the branch, get a tender, and either her or her husband starts dating a socialite famous for being famous so that their family name gets into the tabloids and earns them sympathy and derision in equal measure from the skinner-loving South African public. When you work for this madam, you are not a helper, domestic worker, au pair or whatever fancy name people come up with for cleaning the house, cooking and feeding the children. Here, you are The Maid or The Nanny.

You only work for this madam when you first arrive in the city, otherwise err, never. Your best day working for this madam is your day off or the day you leave. The poor-white madam will try to get you to do as much work as possible for as little money as she can give you. That is because she cannot really afford a domestic helper, but because she believes she is still a madam and there must be a black woman cleaning up for her and hers, she hires a maid anyway. If she is younger, it is because she really does need the help. She just cannot afford it. Apart from where she stays, you will also know this madam because of her washed-out hair that has been bleached too many times. Her salon visit occurs on special occasions when there is extra money. She wears drawstring pants, tracksuit pants, and T-shirts a lot. She seems to buy all her clothes from PEP Stores or at the clothing section of Pick n Pay Hyper. You know this because the clothes are all really No-name brands. She may wear lipstick when she is going to the shops, but because she does not have full lips, it always makes her look mean.

If the madam is under the age of 50, she is a teacher at a pre-school where most middle-class black parents send their children so that they can believe there are high standards because their children are being taught by a white woman. The black parent will never ask what qualifications this poor-white woman has. She has the most important qualification of all: a white skin. And if there are some poor-white children at the nursery school to play with the black woman's child, all the better. Mrs Ferreira or Mrs de Villiers is known to hit the children on the knuckles with a ruler or a duster because she does not really enjoy her job, but what does it matter if the children are being taught by a white woman? And she needs the job as she has to pay her 'nanny'.

She is married to her high-school sweetheart – the star rugby player at her high school who never reached his full rugby potential because she got pregnant and they had a shotgun wedding (he has never stopped resenting her for it); or her older brother's high-school buddy. You know he resents her because every Friday or Saturday when he gets drunk, he starts yelling and telling her about it. The neighbours will call the police who will come and calm him down or threaten to arrest him.

Your madam and her husband live in a flat where they have learnt to nod at the black people who live in the same building and call the police on them. When you work for her, you wake up in the morning and get the child/children ready. They do not eat breakfast at home as food is served at the crèche. The old car that has seen better days goes with the baas who works in the factory and you have to walk the madam to crèche so that her peers can see that she has a maid. You will probably have one child on your back and another in a pram with one problematic wheel. During the weekend, the children like playing with the little black children.

If the madam is over 50, she likely does not work. She and her husband inherited their apartheid house from their late ma or pa. Life passed her by. She does not understand how her loser husband failed to take advantage of apartheid and she is therefore very bitter. What makes her and her husband more bitter is when they have a cheeky black neighbour who drives a BMW. You know this because you see the scowl on both their faces when the car drives in and out. Or when they throw words like 'tenderpreneurs' upon sighting the neighbour's car in your presence. This madam will usually not have you stay in as all her children are still staying at home and doing some manual labour at one of the local factories – not because they are qualified but because some white foreman who worked with their father and now feels sorry for the children of the *volk*, gave them a job.

Sometimes her children have children and the house is very full. So there is a lot of washing and cleaning for the two or three days a week she will ask you to come through. Sometimes you think she even asks her friends to bring their clothes on laundry days. Her sons and husband's clothes are usually greasy and grimy from the factory work. If the husband is retired, then he also works part-time as either a plumber, electric repair man or a cab driver. When working as a plumber or electric repair man, he is said to be really good at his job but he usually charges the black neighbours a higher fee for doing the work. The black neighbours never try to negotiate because they do not want the white man to think they cannot afford it although the black neighbours' helper told you that they still have not paid her the wages for last month.

If you end up being a live-in helper because you

have no relatives in the city that you can stay with and because she says she needs someone full-time and you are desperate for a job, you will regret it very much. When you arrive, she will give you a metal cup and a plate. Although some of those plates are chipped, you are not supposed to use the same utilities as those of the family members. She will also give you a hot plate so you can cook your own food. You will be given rules. Many rules. And it is only desperation that keeps you staying. Because you need a job. "No boyfriends, no friends, no children, no this and that." You wonder as you listen whether you have just agreed to slavery. But you stay because you need the money.

Your schedule entails waking up early in the morning to get the grandchildren ready for school. The children do not wash every day or they wash just before they go to bed so it is a matter of helping them put on their uniforms and getting them to eat breakfast. When there is a bit of money, the children will eat cereal. Most of the time though, they have mealie meal porridge like black children do, or oats. Then you start cleaning. What is funny about the homes of these working-class madams is that no matter how much cleaning you do, the house is never completely clean. The tiles are stained and/or coming off in certain places. The curtains look shabby. There is a calendar of the Blue Bulls and maybe even two stuffed blue sacks hanging on the veranda, in case you forget that this is Blue Bulls' territory. There is also a Blue Bulls' flag and in the homes of the really conservative madam, there is an old apartheid flag. A faded photograph of Koos de la Rey taken from an old copy of *Die Burger* or *The Citizen* takes pride of place. There is a sofa somewhere that's broken but was going to be repaired, yet it is still used, and a shell of a car – Ford Zephyr or some such old make. There is also never a lawn or flowers to be found out in the yard, just sparse patches of grass. And gnomes. Lots and lots of garden gnomes. Where do they get them?

The kitchen has an old fridge which seems to have been bought many years ago when fridges were still called ice boxes, but because the husband is a plumber, it always gets fixed when it stops working. There is, however, a piece of cloth that stays at the bottom of the fridge that you have to squeeze water out of at least five times a day because the fridge leaks. Inside the fridge there is always a supply of boerewors and packets of chicken pieces from Shoprite.

If this madam is generous enough to give you food, it is usually a bag of mealie meal. No meat, no money for vegetables, nothing. Just mealie meal for *pap*. One is never clear whether she thinks black domestic workers eat *pap* without anything else. And yet, when there are little children in the house, they always seem to come to your *khaya* when you go on your break to make some tea or for lunch. These children are always hungry, but they must *voetsek* because your children are starving too. They always follow you to your cottage but they soon learn a single Zulu word, '*sukha*'. It's the word you throw at them just before you close your door so you can cook and eat without their hungry eyes on you.

Sometimes the son-in-law is also staying there because he and their daughter are 'going through a rough patch' financially. It is then that you shake your head. What kind? How can a mother-in-law stay under the same roof as her son-in-law for such a long time at her house? But they do these poor whites, shame. On Fridays and Saturdays, they even drink their Klipdrift and Coke together and are nice to each other before they start fighting. "You are not a real man, you can't even look after your family," the mother-in-law may say.

"Ag nee ma, if you daughter wasn't so lazy and was also doing something, we would be able to get our own place and save a little money," the son-in-law will reply.

The mother will shake her head and curse. "Forty years I have been with pa over there. Never worked in my life and he looks after me. We even bought this house on the money he saved. A real man looks after his family."

The son-in-law will pull out the best defence he can. "But you know they cut my hours at the factory. I think they are trying to find a way of letting all of us white boys go. Now they are saying 'we need minimum matric' because they want to employ the darkies. It's this bloody BEE. BEE *se gat, man*."

When you start hearing this as a domestic helper, you should find a way of sneaking out and being very far away. Otherwise they call you. If you were stubborn enough to give them your real name when you arrived – because err well, even if they are white, this is the new South Africa (when will it stop being new?) – they say, "Em-pho" (because they can say *'mampara'* and *'mampoer'* properly but somehow they fail to say Mpho). Or if you were not stubborn enough and you gave them your white name, they will say, 'So Trinity," and then you know it is coming. "What do you think of this BEE thing? Do you think your fellow blacks without qualifications should be given jobs because of BEE? Heh? Isn't that reverse racism? It's that Em-beki and Zuma. Mandela would never have allowed it."

If you are not South African, say you are from Lesotho, then madam, her husband, son or son-in-law will tell you how "the black South Africans are not as hard working as your people, they are lazy and yet they get jobs because of BEE." If you are from Zimbabwe, it's even worse. "This South African government does not learn, Trinity," one of them will say. "They should have learnt from Mugabe. He chased away all the whites and look where your country is now. If Zuma wants to chase us out with his BEE, this country will become another Zimbabwe, you watch." None of them actually care what you think, so you generally say something non-committal and leave. When you leave, the conversation will either go on fantasising about the time when things were better and how they are saving money to go to Australia, or the daughter will come and complain, after pouring herself a double tot of Klip and some Coke, that her husband managed to buy booze but did not buy disposable nappies for the child, which usually ends up in a physical fight. Often the brothers will tell their sister that she talks too much and will take the side of the brother-in-law. "A man needs to relax sometimes not just get your nagging all the time. You can get some of Marietta's nappies *mos*." Because of this nappy situation, the maid will be called so she can go to one of the spazas and buy nappies at a rand each or, if there was no money left after buying Klip, then it is a week of hell as you have to wash those white cloth nappies that a few people in South Africa still seem to use, but that PEP still sells so that domestic helpers can have more work. Sometimes when you wash them you will use all your strength so that they can tear, but when they get torn, these people will buy some more of the same. Ja neh?

The family car is a bakkie which is handy for the work that the baas does. For the people in the city who may never have been to the house, herewith a moving advertisement for Blue Bulls, complete with horns in the front and blue balls hanging at the bottom of the car in case all the Blue Bulls' stickers are too subtle for their intended audience.

When you work for the poor-white madam, you will leave for three major reasons:

- Because someone you know has found you a better job.
- Because you are tired of all the excuses when it comes to getting your wages. The poor-white madam who always speaks snark of black people and generally is not nice to you, will come and start being nice to you at the end of the month and make excuses for why she cannot pay. When you finally get the money, she will give it to you in dribs and drabs and when the final payment is made just before your next pay she will say something like, "You thought I would not give you your money, didn't you, Em-pho?" in a patronising tone of voice instead of just apologising and ensuring you get your money on time next month.
- Because the husband/sons/son-in-law give you unwanted attention. They do not like black people very much and yet there seems to be some strange fascination with black sexuality with these males. It starts with making sexually suggestive statements in your presence or asking you blatantly how 'you black women like it'. Sometimes they will pinch your bum when the madam or the daughter/daughter-in-law is not looking. When you look at them to tell them you do not like it, they will have a look of innocence on their face like they have not done anything. Weekends

are the worst. It is then that they will come knocking on your door when they are drunk. And that is when you pretend to be fast asleep or not there and you also begin to understand why the little town of Excelsior in the Free State became so famous.

The Liberal Middle-Class White Madam

To black people, she is rich. To white people, she is middle-class. Her husband is a silk, a doctor or a marketing executive. There are two cars, maybe three, in their garage. One for him usually something stable that says, 'I am trustworthy' like a Mercedes E-Class. She stays in Parktown, Linden, Rosebank or Kew. Middle-class neighbourhoods that border on wealthy neighbourhoods. There are some well-heeled suburbs in the south but she will not stay there. It is not in keeping with the image she is trying to portray, as her friends would have to pass through poor neighbourhoods when coming to visit her. She has a Range Rover for the school runs with the children, and if they have another vehicle, it is possibly a caravan for those camping trips to the Drakensberg when baas insists that everyone takes a holiday to be 'in touch with nature' and everyone gets back grumpy because they hated not having reception for their Facebook Status Updates and it was like so lame, like in touch with nature, whatever. You have minimal chance of being employed by this madam if you are a younger woman than her. The requirement for employment is that you must be the same age as her or older. It is ideal if you have children the same age as her or older. That way she and her husband can practise their liberal credentials. She may have inherited you from some French/Italian expatriate wife whose husband was her husband's boss working on a contract in South Africa. The friend sent a group email:

> *"Sadly we are leaving for Paris/Rome/Venice and though we would love to, we cannot take our brilliant Malawian cook (Chimwemwe), Gladness our house-help, our driver Thomas, or our green-fingered Zimbabwean gardener Whatmore. All four have been with us for the five years we have been in South Africa and are hardworking, reliable, very honest and able to communicate well in English (and Chimwemwe makes gourmet French meals that would make many a chef in Franschhoek envious). They have never moaned or fussed when asked to work overtime or on a weekend. We could rely on them 100% when we travelled to take care of our darling little poodles and our son – their meals, school rounds, and even help*

with the homework. They have been a part
of our family and will be dearly missed and
we hope they can be a part of yours, too."

The middle-class madam took you on. She thinks this may count as a plus for her husband (because of his boss) and besides the old domestic worker that raised her and who she inherited from her parents has been saying she wants to retire and die at home somewhere in rural KwaZulu-Natal or in the Free State. This is the opportunity for the madam to get a new helper and let go of her trusted Sweetie, who is like a family member to her. What better way than to inherit someone reliable from her husband's boss's wife? She cannot afford all the four employees though, so in the end she will ask for the house-help, Gladness. "Oh I really do not need a driver. Mornings when I take the children to school, is my time to bond with them. And I am quite a good cook myself. I make a mean quiche, Jeremy tells me." The French wife of the boss will smile knowingly and attempt not to raise her eyebrows, because she knows exactly how much our middle-class white madam's husband earns.

"Gladness, the children can come and see you here anytime. Anytime, you hear?" she says speaking to you very slowly, as though you are deaf and need to read her lips because, err, you will understand English much better when she speaks slowly. She likes a good sob story, so it will be good if the father of your children abandoned you and you have been looking after the children alone. Or better yet, you are a Christian widow. Both these situations reduce the chances of your bringing a prospective criminal under the guise of a boyfriend. "My husband is an atheist but I am agnostic, do you know what that means, Gladness?" she will ask you. "But we believe in living and letting live," she will say. If you are hired by her, you are likely to stay employed by her for a long time. Madam always seems to be busy. Her day begins after you have ensured her two children have had breakfast. Toast and tea with no butter for the ten-year-old girl who does ballet because, "I do not want to be fat." Cereal for the fourteen-year-old boy. And oats for the six-year-old boy, "because Sweetie said oats are good for a growing boy." You want to say, "Sweetie *se gat*," but you do not because you are still new here, the money is good, as is your cottage, and besides, Sweetie is old enough to be your mother's younger sister.

Madam has coffee and biscotti or just a cup of coffee in the morning. Her husband has continental breakfast during the week and full English on Saturday. You worked for the French and they too, had this continental breakfast but you are never quite sure which continent is being talked about with fruit and cold meats. Madam ushers the children in her Range, kisses her husband at the door and removes lint from his suit jacket just before he walks to his car. Just how much lint can be on a man's suit, you wonder? She does this every day.

She wears a different high-end gym kit every day and puts her sunglasses above her forehead although the sun is not quite shining yet. A busy woman, this madam. When she returns around ten, she would have dropped the children at school, gone to the gym, and will be back to shower and have a light breakfast. That is if she is not coming through to change so that she can go to the salon or to another meeting. She is in the School Development Association at her children's school. She has to attend meetings, meet friends for coffee, pick up the children from school or attend their sports meets, go to a book launch or her husband's cocktail party at work. "Oh dear, is that the time? I really must go. Don't forget to feed the children. Make sure they are all in bed by nine, Gladness, okay?"

When it comes to cleaning the home, you are lucky. There is a dishwasher in the kitchen. There is a washing machine and a dryer for the laundry. There is – no other way to say it – a Hoover for the fully carpeted floors. Because madam understands that Johannesburg winters are too cold for tiles. The children's rooms have duvets so there is minimal work in bed-making. "This is your home, Gladness. Make sure you eat whenever you are hungry," she says. "You can eat at the cottage off working hours but feel free to eat here when you are working." But you know if you eat more than two slices of bread or put more than three teaspoons of sugar in your tea she will say in an exasperated voice, "The bread is finished already?" or "That much sugar cannot be good for you, Gladness." And when she realises what she has just said because it may hurt her liberal credentials she says, "Oh of course you don't have to go hungry. I did not mean anything by that. You eat, Gladness dear, eat some more." So you always make sure that you have some food at the cottage that you can eat later.

This madam's house is well organised. There is a roster of what should be cooked for dinner every day and what should be packed for the children's lunches the next day. Her husband's suits are charcoal and navy-blue and the shirts are all more or less the same colour.

The husband insists he is a single malt whisky man. He has two glasses of whisky before he has dinner daily and a glass before he goes to bed. The madam says he cannot sleep without some and it helps relax him. Three glasses of three doubles on the rocks. Three ice cubes. Always.

The teenage son smokes marijuana. One Friday when his father and mother have gone to a cocktail party, he has some friends over, including his girlfriend. They bake some biscuits. You taste some. You have three. Then you start feeling as though you are going to die. The world is moving in slow motion. Everything is going wrong. You think you are definitely going to meet your Maker. So you go to this teenage boy and his friends and ask whether they poisoned the biscuits. You tell him you need to go to the hospital before you die. They laugh and say, "Gladness is *irie*." He and his friends say a lot of reggae words because they think it's cool.

You do not remember what happens next. But you think that young boy must have put something bad in your food. The next morning you are woken by him knocking on your door. You are fully clothed on top of your bed and your door is not locked.

"Please do not tell my parents about the cookies yesterday Gladness, please," he begs.

You look at him not quite understanding. And then it dawns, "what was in there? Why are you causing me all these problems at work?" you ask.

This time he does not try to correct your English pronunciation like he always does. "It's not 'wek' Gladness, it's 'work.' Say 'work'." He just says, "Nothing. Please do not say anything to my mom, otherwise I will be grounded forever."

You look at him in a 'what's-in-it-for-me fashion'. And he takes out one hundred rand. A hundred rand? What does he think you can do with a hundred rand? You raise your eyebrow and do not stretch out your hand. Only when he has gone back to his room and come back with five hundred rand do you finally say,

"What cookies. Were there some cookies in the house?"

There is a peculiarity about the liberal middle-class white madam. Although you have never seen them at her house, she loves telling you that she has black friends.

Her husband does not talk much to you beyond saying hello, and asking for his glass of whisky, food or other request. The only time he will put in a word is when they both sit you down and tell you that they feel they need to give back and would like to pay school fees for your children, so can they get the details of the best government school in your hometown. This is a good thing.

What is worrying is when the madam and her husband decide to extend the notion of the Rainbow Nation and reconciliation too far and decide that they want your children to come and stay with you, so that they can put them in the same school as their children. This is worrying because they will try hard to have your children not feel uncomfortable and so will put them in the main house and the madam will drive them to school. You will soon see your children being ashamed of you, and they will never really invite the friends they make home, or when they do you have to stay in the cottage so that you do not embarrass them.

The other worrying thing about the liberal madam is that she is always trying to get you to vote for the DA. She does not say so in such a blatant way. She does it in a way she thinks is subtle. She will tell you, when she comes from Cape Town after accompanying her husband on a business meeting, how pretty it is and how the DA has done such a good job. "It is really so clean, Gladness," she will say enthusiastically. "Not like downtown Johannesburg where people just dump everything everywhere and no-one seems to pick anything up. Sometimes one wonders what we are paying our rates for." Then when it is time to register, she will ask you whether you have registered to vote. If you have not, she will insist on driving with you to register – just so she makes sure that you vote. And then before the elections, she will constantly point out another corrupt scandal by the ANC, "Look, there are more toilets uncovered because of them." "What we need Gladness, is a change. Helen Zille seems to know what she is doing. And she can even speak your language. Do you know that she is the one who investigated the death of Steve Biko? And look at the ANC now. What would Biko say?" Unfortunately for her, even if she goes with you to the polling station on the day of the election, she will not vote with you. Vote DA? Huh. They would probably ban the Domestic Workers Union and the minimum wage because you should just be happy to have a job no matter how little you're earning. And where was the DA when the ANC was freeing you from apartheid? Never.

The good news about the liberal middle-class white

madam though is that she is generally quite decent, will pay you a tolerable salary, and, if you are a decent helper, you will generally stay with her until you decide you want to leave because she is so keen not to cause offence.

Why you will part ways:
- There has been one too many break-ins at their house and they are leaving for Australia/England/Canada.
- The husband fails to get a promotion that he was a shoo-in for, which was given to a black man/woman and there is an offer for another job in Australia/England/Canada.
- Both the husband and wife will not stop calling you and embarrassing you in front of their guests by recounting how, during the first elections, you dropped your ID book in the ballot box instead of the ballot paper. You are tired of laughing along with them at this silly not-so-funny joke.
- She brings you a DA T-shirt and keeps asking, "Why don't you ever wear your DA T-shirt when you go to the shops, Gladness?"
- The husband's name is Tony Leon and he has been made an ambassador to Argentina to get him out of the way so he can stop doing interviews with the liberal white media and antagonising the governing party.
- You are retiring.

- You disagree on how they are spoiling your child. In which case you will probably lose a daughter/son as the child will insist on staying with them, and the madam and baas will guilt you into letting your child stay behind so (s)he can access better opportunities because, "you don't want your child to be a domestic worker like you, do you?"
- The father of your children wants a reunion. He promises he will look after you. You think it is a good idea but you suspect you will regret the decision a few months after you have returned to him.

Ending Notes for Helpers:

And so there you have it, sistahs. There is no way in hell you haven't been hacking through this bunch to find the perfect job, but now you know how to avoid the crazies! Don't say you were not warned.

PART II

"*No good help these days*"

– THE MADAM'S HANDBOOK

The Helpers

Good help is difficult to find these days. As a prospective madam, there are so many landmines you have to deal with in the domestic helpers' sphere. But, what do you do? There are always places to go and things to do and you are willing to admit that, like Karen White, you are not a superwoman. But inviting a stranger into your home is often a problematic thing and you have to be careful. And part of being careful is having some wide brush-strokes so that you have an idea of the helper you may encounter. However different their backgrounds, there are some similarities among many of the helpers. You cannot go around asking, "Who ate my cheese?" The helper did. She also finished the bread, the meat, and the sugar is gone in a week because she used it. And it's not because they are all greedy and want to leave you bankrupt, no. It is plain and simple. Unless you, madam, suffer from some white disease like anorexia, even you would eat more if you stayed at home. Think about it and put yourself in the helper's shoe. She wakes up. Has breakfast. Everyone leaves to go to work or school, and she is left alone. And gets lonely. So what does she do?

Well she does the only thing there is to do. She cleans. Does laundry. And she watches Nollywood. But with great Nollywood comes great eating. One cannot just watch Nollywood without a cup of tea. So your helper will make some tea. If possible it will not be a cup of tea but tea in a teapot so she does not have to just get up and warm more water the whole day. But as most people, except obsessively figure-conscious madams know, tea cannot be drunk *nje*. So the helper may make some sandwiches. There is a whole roll of polony in the fridge so what is a little bit for your helper's tea break? So she cuts off some slices, adds some cheese, and goes and sits down to watch another movie 'sterring' Ramsey Noah, Desmond Elliot, or that very funny Nkem Owoh alongside Genevieve, Rita Dominic, or that Moji Olaiya who wants to give all Nollywood actresses a bad name by saying that they play sex games on set with the actors. *Nccc*!

So anyway madam, to save yourself from the "who ate my cheese?" situation, the ideal would be to have your helper staying in a cottage and she can buy her own food so that there will be no justification for eating the food in your fridge and 'finishing it' as your stingy person likes to claim. If your house is not big enough and does not have a cottage, say you live in one of those town house complexes where each room is three metres by two metres in Midrand, Ormonde or Ridgeway, your next plan is to tell her what is off-limits to her. "*Ausi*," you could say, "the polony/cheese is for the children's sandwiches." You also need to inform her that she can only have one egg for breakfast. But you do this not in a "I am a stingy madam" tone of voice but more of a "I am a caring madam" tone of voice. You do this by informing her how, for breakfast there was some aunt of yours who used to fry three eggs, with six slices of bread and four teaspoons of sugar in her tea. And how one day she had a stroke and cannot move/is dead because when you took her to hospital they said the stroke was caused by sugar and a heart attack. Please do not say lofty words like, "she was diabetic and also had a cardiac arrest." You want to keep it simple so that your helper begins to fear what eating too much bread, sugar and eggs may do to her.

Now: you may, or may not have an aunt who had a stroke (if you are any of the blacks – African, Coloured, Indian – due to a large extended family, you do), that is beside the point. The point is that, you want to save on the money you use on groceries now that you have a domestic helper. At the worst, after telling your helper this story, she will eat four slices of bread, have two eggs and three sugars in her tea. Which is quite some saving when you consider that every other day she is having her egg and bread from your neighbour's house because their helper and she have become friends. You will need to know that whatever helper you get, they will come with their pros and cons. There are five basic categories of helpers for a South African madam of whatever race: **The City Helper, The Rural Helper, The Zimbabwean, The Mosotho,** and **The Malawian Helper.** As a madam, you will have to choose carefully depending on your needs. While your friend might swear by her Zimbabwean helper, someone from rural Eastern Cape, KZN, North West, Limpopo or Mpumalanga may suit you better. Know your facts and then make your decision.

The City Helper

She may be younger or older.

IF SHE IS YOUNGER:

She will come to you through an employment agency. She is a teenage mother with matric, is orphaned, or just some young woman who failed matric and needs something to keep her going. If she comes from a particularly good domestic workers' agency, she has been trained to cook, clean and look after the child/children. She will do all this well. She will help the child/children with the homework and will not have to be constantly told what to do. Most madams like to complain that domestic workers have to be told everything, but you have no fear on that account with this one. She will predict your needs before you have stated them.

Children's shoes need polishing? Do not worry. The young city helper has got you covered.

You need your suit to be picked up from the cleaners? Before you state it, the young city helper will say to you as you are walking out of the door, "Eh *ausi*, I think you forgot to leave the receipt and the money for the dry cleaners. Am I not supposed to pick up your clothes from the dry cleaners?"

She will be indispensable and you will find no fault with her.

Your city helper watches reruns of *Generations, Rhythm City, Isidingo* and *Scandal*. When it is in season, she is more likely to watch *Big Brother Africa* than Nollywood, although she watches Nollywood once in a while. She also watches *Top Billing*, either with you or as re-runs and she has seen those houses that both of you can only dream of. She has grown up seeing how Nandipha in *Isidingo* started as a domestic helper and then became a top television presenter. Or how Khethiwe was this ignorant rural domestic helper with a crush on uButi Tau who not only managed to attract his attention for some time (although she lost it again, damn Karabo), but eventually managed to own a business as well as being a copywriter at a leading advertising agency. She buys copies of *Drum* and *Move* and knows how to have a Foschini style or a Beyonce or Rihanna look for R800. She could teach you or me a thing or two.

It is then that seeds of discontent begin to be seen. Your trusted helper who came to you grateful to have a job, now realises she cannot have all the looks she wants with the money that you are paying her. This young woman is a clevah from the city and she knows that she is your au pair, cook and personal assistant rolled into one; although you are only paying her the minimum wage as suggested by the Department of Labour (what does the Minister of Labour know anyway? You overheard her ask one of her friends this question on the phone. The Minister of Labour should try to live on R2 500 a month and let's see how they like it). She looks at you and thinks, "there, but for my parents' lack of money for university, is me." She too would like to have an iPhone instead of this Nokia from '20 *Voetsek*'. Some of the friends she went to school with have one. Another is even driving a Mini Cooper thanks to her sugar daddy from varsity. In short: she aspires to be you.

When you ask her to do something, she will start doing things just a little slower than normal. She is not as bubbly as she used to be. She is just that bit slower. Sometimes she burns the dinner and you are never quite sure whether to chastise her because you are not quite sure whether she did it deliberately.

You let her go when:
• You see her Facebook profile and she is wearing your outfits in her album.

- Your bottle of Ruperts and Rothschild wine is just not at the same level it was the last time you drank it.
- She gets pregnant on one of her days off and you cannot afford to go without a helper for the time she is expected to take maternity leave.
- She laughs too loudly at all those jokes that your husband/partner cracks that you feel are dry and need a little water, and you catch him when he does not know you are looking, drooling at her nubile body.

Sometimes she is the one who will let you go. That is because she has saved enough money for the Quest Call Centre course she always wanted to attend and she is aiming for something better. You shall next hear from her when she answers your phone when you call FNB, ABSA, Nedbank or Standard Bank to complain about odd transactions on your card that you had nothing to do with. Or to question why your overdraft was not increased. Which is not the type of information you want your former helper to know about.

IF SHE IS OLDER:

She will work tirelessly and you will wonder what you ever did without gogo. She is a widow who probably worked *emakishini* before she got married. When she got married, she continued working but this time on a part-time level as she would take in washing from the madams in the different suburbs pre-1994. After 1994, she stopped most of that to take care of her ailing husband. He has died now. And following behind him sometime later, were three of her five children.

She now needs work so she can look after the grandchildren that were left behind.

She loves her grandchildren and is great with your children. She also has the street smarts and you are allowed to act like you have not noticed every now and again when she is drinking her papsak in a cup of tea. Or when she takes a bit of the brandy or vodka in the house. She cannot, unfortunately, assist with homework unless she is a retired teacher, but it is a small price to pay for the way that there is a place for everything and everything in its place in your house. You will also need to understand that the older city helper does not work during weekends. That is because weekends are for funerals and she also needs to check on whether everything is smooth-running at home with her grandchildren.

The older city helper understands that she needs to give you and your partner space. If you are a single woman, she will wink when you have more than one boyfriend and will exchange with you, in a whispery voice, tales of when she too was a hot mama who was getting courted by all these jazz singers that you have heard about back in Sophiatown/Alexandra. In some ways she is like your mother. But she is way cooler than your mother as she does not tell you what to do. That is the cornerstone of your relationship with her. She knows you are an employer and she is the employee, but that you will respect her on account of her age so you will correct her gently for any mistakes. And because she has done this work before, she will take it in the spirit that your criticism is meant to be given.

You will not let this old lady go. She is such a gem. She will only leave because she tells you she is too tired, or her grandchildren are old enough and do not need any help, or your children are grown up enough and do not really need her.

You will be sorry to see her leave.

The Rural Helper

*T*he rural South African helper generally works for
  Africans.

You get her through one of two ways. From your
mother or from your mother-in-law.

MOTHER'S HELPER:

Your mother hears that you have let yet another
domestic worker go. She is the sixth helper you have let
go in 18 months. Mother then calls one of her cousins
from Qua Qua, Mount Frere (insert your alleged home
town that you have never been to or have only ever
gone for *umsebenzi*). Your mother's cousin says she
knows just the person who will work hard, is loyal,
needs the money and, and, and. She has even worked
for about four white madams on the white side of your
alleged home town before. Your mother does not see fit

to tell you all this. Neither does she see fit to ask your aunt why this woman worked for so many madams if she is so loyal, hard-working and everything else. In the next 24 hours, you will have to e-wallet your guest-employee (so called because she is family so is not fully any employee) some money for transport. Forty-eight hours later, you will be picking up this woman – your cousin – from Park Station when she arrives.

You know you will not have a normal employer/ employee relationship as she calls you 'mkhaya, mzala' or if she is not as shy as she should be on first meeting you, 'cuz'. Whether shy or not, in the car as you drive to your home, she will not be embarrassed to show her gratitude. She will tell you how grateful she is that you have done this for her. "*Mzala*, I hope one day I can do the same for you. You have saved my life. My children can now eat," she will say effusively to your embarrassment. Then she will tell you all the problems that are on her side of the family. The brother who got arrested. The young sister who is doing a '*vat 'n sit*' with the boy from across the street who is not even the father of any of her three children; And how he beats her if she does not bring the children's *papgeld* for him to drink every month. So now you know, according to her version of things, she is the breadwinner and you have to pay her well. If you are married, she will also take on this sort of familiarity with your husband and children. They are her nieces and her nephews after all and he is her *s'bali* even though you had never heard of her before that fateful phone call from your mother.

Her work is not always up to standard. When it comes to cleaning, she has a habit of cleaning the common area and not moving the seats. When you politely tell her that she is not cleaning properly, she sulks because "I have been cleaning my mother's house since I was a little girl" and feels insulted that you would tell her how to clean. Additionally, she cannot believe that a family member would talk to her this way.

It is hoped, madam, that your husband/partner does not have an inferiority complex if you earn more than he does or get a promotion at any point in time after your *mkhaya/mzala* arrives, because she may well start taking 'care of him' very well. She will serve her *s'bali* while kneeling with just the right amount of coyness. And she has just the right amount of playfulness and respect that a weak male with an inferiority complex may fall for.

You will know that it is time to let her go and you will drop her with her *mamkhulu/mamncane* (your mother) when she starts advising you about your girls' night out and questioning why or how you are taking care of your husband. Your mother will only be forgiving if you tell her how much her relative (always be sure to emphasise, 'your relative') was cosy-ing up to your man. It is then that your mother will respond by telling you how she always knew that this girl's mother had not taught them properly. It is now that your mother may tell you how the mother of the cousin you did not know you had never taught her children anything. How they have no morals. How they all have different fathers. And how the cousin you did not know you had, "is just like her mother".

Another reason you may have to let go of your cousin's helper is that you find out that the phone bill at home is very high. When Telkom sends the bill, there are various phone calls to your alleged home town. When you question this and justify, "both my husband and I use our phones at work so there is no reason why this bill should be so high," she will decide you are unfairly accusing her since she too, was using the phone at her place of employment.

If you do not let her go because of the phone bill but instead threaten her with deductions from her salary if the next phone bill is high, she may do something unbelievably cruel that will ensure that you do fire her. For example, a child will pull a boiling kettle and burn him- or herself. You and your husband will arrive home an hour later and find the child howling. When you ask her why she did not call you, she will respond, "I did not have airtime and you told me not to use the phone."

In this instance, your mother will owe you and may be very nice to you and offer to watch the children for a while until you get the next helper.

Say no.

And get someone from an agency, even if temporarily.

You are too old to have your mother staying in your house indefinitely, madam.

Mother-in-Law's Helper:

She is also known as *Jane Bond 007*. Or the spy who cleaned for me. And you, madam, are that naive woman who believes that your mother-in-law loves you so much that when you once again do not have a helper, she will send one of her cousins or nieces to come and help you out. Beware. She is just sending someone so that she gets a report back on how you are treating her little boy. Like the helper from your mother, she too will come and familiarise with the family. In this instance though, you are supposed to be the humble one because you are a *makoti*.

You will know that you have problems the first time that your mother-in-law visits after Jane Bond has been working for you. It is then that you see your *mamzala* not only sitting in the kitchen eating with the helper because, "we are just catching up about home/ the television is too loud for me", but you will also notice your *mamzala* helping her wash the dishes. Thus hinting that you may be abusing her niece.

She brings some stability to the home as she is strict with the children. She ensures homework is done as well as other domestic chores. You will, however, sometimes question what you are paying her for since she will find a way of getting your children to do some of the stuff that she should be doing. When she arrives, even if you think she is a terrible cook, help her along the way and show her the spices. This is because if you do not and she sees you putting spices in the food as you cook, she will send a Please-call to your *mamzala* who will come charging and questioning about your habits of bewitching her son. Complete with 'proof' of the stuff that the helper saw you putting in the food. She will want to spade the children (give them enemas), give them cod liver oil, and all those things that you thought you had avoided after your *mamzala* left the house when she was visiting. "So you do not want me to spade the children? I guess they are your children but if they start getting ill, you cannot say I did not tell you." The children love her though as she tells them some interesting stories of their father when he was growing up.

If you avoid letting her go because, good-natured madam that you are (and you are tired of hiring new helpers who have to learn your ways all over again) after the spices incident, you may still find yourself having to let her go when you find out that she is beating the children. This may cause conflict as your husband believes children must be hit. "I grew up getting beaten, look at me. I did not turn out so badly, did I? You want us to spoil these children?" He will ask angrily. It is only after she leaves that you will find the extent of her damage between you and your husband's relatives.

Your mother-in-law now has all the files on how you do not take the children to church or how you drink too much. Your mother-in-law, being full of decorum, will of course not tell you. She will tell your sister/brother-in-law who will let it all out one day when they are drunk and you refuse to pay school fees for their son/daughter. "We always knew you were a witch/bitch. Even our mother does not think you are good enough for our brother. MamThembu told her how much you spend on alcohol every week and yet you cannot even pay for your own nephew/niece's school fees. *Ja sies.* You Xhosa/Zulu/Swati/Pedi/Venda/Sotho chicks are sluts. Just eating my brother's money."

Your mother-in-law will only be okay with your having let her relative go when she finds out she was knocked up by your next-door neighbour. She will not be able to believe that this cousin/niece of hers did not even have respect for her son. When she expresses her disappointment, it is also your time to redeem yourself. You can start telling her whatever bad things you can think about so that she does not believe whatever things her cousin/niece told her. After all, you have the moral high ground on account of her pregnancy by the neighbour.

The wine?

Oh, the bottle was indeed finished in one evening but you do not, in fact, drink. You used it for cooking the stew. Johannesburg winters are cold and need rich stews. And your dear husband and her dear son loves those stews so much.

Henceforth you must be careful.

When you drink, make sure it is gin and juice, or mimosas so she assumes you are drinking orange juice.

Or Irish coffees.

Your mother-in-law may be like a mother to you but she is not YOUR mother. You do not want her to think you are a lush. Unless you drink together.

The Zimbabwean Helper

*T*he Zimbabwean helper has a colourful first name and you are never sure whether the name is a verb, adverb, pronoun, noun or something literally translated from isiNdebele/Shona into English. She is named Loveness, Nomatter, Memory, Silence or maybe Puzzle.

You are a middle-class African, Coloured, Indian or white madam still embarrassed about your government's hand in the Zimbabwean plight. You admit it, although you would not have then, yes. Thabo was a better President than Zuma but what the heck was quiet diplomacy? You are sorry for quiet diplomacy. And you are sorry for what your fellow South Africans did to the Zimbabweans (and Mozambicans. And Malawians. But mostly Zimbabweans. Because we do not want to become another Zimbabwe). So when Nomatter rings your doorbell just when you need a helper the most and tells you her story... When Loveness tells you how she crossed the Limpopo River for a better life in South Africa with a piece of chicken tied at the end a pole so that the crocodiles would go for the chicken and not her... Or you learn how Puzzle had to pay a *malaicha* (one of those illegal cross-border traffickers) all the money she had left to come to this land of opportunity, you decide there and then that it is your duty to help her. After all, you too need help. So you hire Memory.

At first Silence is very hard-working. She cooks. She cleans. She helps the children with the homework. She used to be a teacher. She says. Sometimes she has papers permitting her to work. At other times, she has a visa but she is still trying to sort her papers out. You do all you can to help. She needs a letter for Home Affairs? You write it. Your child/children like her. You like her.

On her day off she goes to visit her aunt in Hillbrow.

One day you come home drunk with one of your crazy friends. You have withdrawn money for your child/children's school fees at the private school he/she/they attend. You hide the money. Your crazy, drunk friend sleeps over at your house. Your boyfriend calls you while she is sleeping for a 'booty call' not too far away. You leave a note for your friend and go to your boyfriend's house.

This is normal behaviour for you so you do not leave a note for your Zimbabwean helper.

In the morning when you come back home to drop the child/children at school, your friend has gone.

You cannot find the money for the school fees.

You call your crazy friend to check.

"Sorry hun, I did not see any money. Have you asked your helper?" she asks, throwing in an Americanism to show how cosmopolitan she is.

Your friend is an artist. Maybe she is a poet, an actress or a musician. She does not always have a constant income. But surely she would not steal from you? She has always told you when she did not have money. And you have always helped when you could. She knows you are a single mother. And your babydaddy is not paying child support. Could she have? You are not certain but maybe she is right. Maybe you need to ask your helper.

You call your Zimbabwean helper. She might have taken the money. It is a substantial amount of money and it would probably assist her suffering family in Zimbabwe.

"Loveness, did you see the money that I left in my bedroom?" you ask.

"No. I was waiting for you to get back before I cleaned your bedroom," she answers.

"But the bedroom was open when I got here. Are you sure you did not take the money?" you ask again, sounding a tad accusatory.

"No, *sisi*. I would never take money without agreeing with you first."

You still suspect her.

And she continues doing her work.

When you pay her at the end of the month, she leaves for her day off, in your absence. She does not return. She leaves you an injured note on her pillow about how she has never been accused of stealing and how "we Zimbabweans are hard-working and although we are poor, we are dignified." It is an eloquently written letter. As you would expect from a former school teacher. Meanwhile, you have just taken an overdraft from your bank to pay for the money that mysteriously disappeared. You are still unsure whether it was your artist friend or the Zimbabwean helper who stole the money. Maybe the sense of injury was false?

And then one day when you decide to wear your Ferragamo shoes for an important function, voila. You find the money. You remember that you put it there before you went to your boyfriend's house that drunken night because you did not want it to be stolen. After all, you had that starving artist friend, and a starving Zimbabwean helper in your house.

You feel terrible.

You immediately call your friend and tell her you have found the money.

She laughs and takes it in good humor. You are unsure whether she knows that you thought she may have been the thief.

You call your Zimbabwean helper.

"The number you have dialled is no longer in service," MTN tells you.

But then one day as you are driving along Louis Botha Avenue, you see her. You beep. She sees your car. She sees that you see her. She walks on and ignores you. There is nowhere for you to park. You would really have liked to say sorry.

You are ashamed. You are just as bad as your countrymen. For, was not your silent accusation a form of Afrophobia? You call your artist friend. "My friend you won't believe this," you say to her. You tell her how *kak* you are feeling. And you offer to buy her a drink so she can commiserate with you about how you treated your wonderful Zimbabwean helper.

She agrees.

You drink, cry in your wine, and when you wake up, you feel worse. It is the hangover.

The Mosotho Helper

Johannesburg middle-class madams of whatever race swear by them. They tell you how hard working these women are, how respectful, and how loyal they are. And they are all that.

But do not make the mistake of hiring someone from the Free State. The helper from the Free State is already covered under the city/rural South African helper. She may consider herself a Mosotho too, but as far as helpers go, she, madam, is not the genuine thing. The real, honest to God, Allah, Buddha, the ancestors, or no god (because we members of the Rainbow Nation celebrate all religions even those who claim they do not believe in She, the Omnipotent One) is a Mosotho from Lesotho.

While it is true that the former Basutoland is fully bordered by South Africa, you do not have to find out which is the closest border to your home to go and recruit this beloved of helpers. No. All you need to do is ask one of your friends who always brags about her fantastic Mosotho helper. She is bound to have a cousin who is looking for a job. She tells you that she is her sister. If you are white, you will be taken aback when five years down the line you find out that they just come from the same village, when you drive her to a funeral because you are yearning for an adventure in Africa but close enough to South Africa. If you identify as African, Indian, Coloured and you are taken aback then you need to hand in your race card right now. You have become too much of a Clever Black and are not in touch with what it means to be black. It is her sister. They are from the same clan mos.

Unlike your rural cousin that you did not know you had, you do not need to send money to Lesotho for your friend's helper's sister. And your friend says she is never quite sure whether there is some stokvel where money is kept for men and women who are going to work in South Africa. Your friend could be onto something. Twenty-four hours after you confirm your request to her sister, your Mosotho helper will arrive.

And yes. She is everything that your friends said she would be and more.

She cleans. Well.

She cooks. Well.

She minds the infant and/or toddler. Well.

Unfortunately she does not speak English as well, so she may not be able to assist with the homework.

If you speak Northern Sotho, Southern Sotho, or Setswana, you should be able to communicate pretty well.

If you are a Nguni-speaking, Joburg-residing character, the seSotho you have picked up in the streets should be able to help.

If you are Coloured, Indian or white and do not feel that you need to learn another language aside from English and/or Afrikaans "all my friends speak English and my poor cousins speak Afrikaans", then you will have to make do with sign language. We just hope you are good at it. Because your infant or toddler will learn to say 'mme' and speak the language before any of the languages you claim as 'your own'. She is just that good.

You will not let her go. She will leave because she is getting married. If she is elderly, she will leave because her daughter is coming. Either to replace her or to replace you.

Because she is just that good.

The Malawian Helper

*T*his is not the type of helper for just anybody *nje*. The Malawian helper is a special type of helper. If you are a middle-class madam, forget it. You will not get this one. The Malawian helper is for the upper middle-class. If you are a madam, you need to be knocking on the door written 'rich' and about to enter. No. Not nouveau riche. Upper middle-class. You have known the smell of money all your life. You have played polo all your life. The only difference is that the horses belong to your aunt. But you are part of the set.

The jet-setting set. London. Cape Town. Joburg.

Because having a Malawian helper is never about the Malawian helper. It is about you. You need to fit your Malawian helper's requirements.

If you do fit the Malawian helper's requirements, then you may need to know your helper's profile.

Your Malawian helper is not a woman. He is

a Malawian man who may or may not be called Chimwemwe.

He will require a maid to clean the house.

And you will get him a maid to clean the house.

That is because he is such a brilliant cook.

You want to have little dinner parties as often as possible just so you can show off Chimwemwe's cooking. His bream is to die for. Must be something he learnt on the shores of Lake Malawi. He will not let the maid polish the silver though. She may not know how to do it properly, so he polishes the silver himself.

Chimwemwe is always in his khaki or white uniform when he is in the house. And he has an apron to go with it.

In the garden, Chimwemwe wears an overall. He also has green fingers (there is a reason why the good weed is called Malawi Gold, you know). So, although you may have a maid in the house for cleaning (cleaning the house is women's work), you will not require a gardener for your garden. And your garden has never looked more lush. What he may need is an assistant, ideally a hard-working Zimbabwean to come and help in the garden twice or thrice a week when there is a lot of digging to be done.

He also drives you or the children – because Chimwemwe is not just any average, ordinary helper. He is a manservant. That means butler, chef, driver and concierge.

He does not do homework.

You will have to get an au pair for that.

Chimwemwe has one bad habit. If you do not smoke, you may not appreciate that he needs to smoke some weed every now and again. If you are one of those upper-middle-class madams, then you will absolutely love Chimwemwe as he will procure the best stuff for you but will have the delicacy of never smoking *with* you (he just rolls your joints or sets up your bong).

You will lose Chimwemwe when there is some global economic meltdown and you realise that you can get one employee for the price that you are paying Chimwemwe and all his assistants. But this also means that you will be looked down on by members of your set.

"The Brooks had to let go of that wonderful cook of theirs. Yes. It appears times are indeed difficult. Shhh, Lauri is walking in now. Let's talk about this later."

You will know they were talking about you because of the pitying looks on their faces.

You may also lose Chimwemwe because he was head-hunted by one of your friends. That one who has always been competing with you since primary school and who you do not like but must keep because she is important for your image. Chimwemwe is loyal enough to tell you about the head-hunting, but since your husband thinks you pay him way too much and that you are being frivolous, you lose him anyway.

Ending Notes for Madams:

*I*t's true what they say, they don't come like they used to, fresh from the farms, willing to do your bidding and all that. And even when you've done EVERYTHING to make them feel like family, they run off and come back with CCMA notes months later when UIF hasn't paid up. But clutch this note to your chest, ladies. You never know when you might need it!